T0209521

BITTERNESS

A Snare of the
FOWLER

MARK POGUE

WESTBOW
PRESS®
A DIVISION OF THOMAS NELSON
& ZONDERVAN

WestBow Press books may be ordered through booksellers or by contacting:

WestBow Press
A Division of Thomas Nelson & Zondervan
1663 Liberty Drive
Bloomington, IN 47403
www.westbowpress.com
1 (866) 928-1240

Because of the dynamic nature of the Internet, any web addresses or links contained in this book may have changed since publication and may no longer be valid. The views expressed in this work are solely those of the author and do not necessarily reflect the views of the publisher, and the publisher hereby disclaims any responsibility for them.

Any people depicted in stock imagery provided by Getty Images are models, and such images are being used for illustrative purposes only. Certain stock imagery © Getty Images.

Unless otherwise indicated, all Scripture taken from the New King James Version®. Copyright © 1982 by Thomas Nelson. Used by permission. All rights reserved.

Scripture quotations are from the ESV® Bible (The Holy Bible, English Standard Version®), copyright © 2001 by Crossway, a publishing ministry of Good News Publishers. Used by permission. All rights reserved.

ISBN: 978-1-9736-7112-1 (sc)
ISBN: 978-1-9736-7114-5 (hc)
ISBN: 978-1-9736-7113-8 (e)

Library of Congress Control Number: 2019910921

Print information available on the last page.

WestBow Press rev. date: 11/13/2019

Contents

Bitterness seems to be all the rage today. We look at the news stations or read publications expressing anger and bitterness over various things in the social scope today. Some circles call it expression. The Bible speaks of bitterness being sin. This book is timely for our world today. Especially timely for those who would like encouragement to overcome anger and bitterness. It affects many avenues of life. It is a snare. In his book "Bitterness A Snare of the Fowler," Mark Pogue details biblically the root of bitterness, the snare of bitterness, but most importantly the grace of God to forgive and restore. With conviction and high esteem that you read this book as it will bear witness of God's love and forgiveness for anyone who has dealt with this subject.

Pastor Dennis Morales
Calvary Chapel Eastvale

0

"The thief does not come except to steal, and to kill, and to destroy. I have come that they may have life, and that they may have it more abundantly.

John 10:10

There are so many people today who are hurting and are so far away from this abundant life that Jesus speaks about here in *John 10:10*. Many are non-believers, but many are believers. As I address in this book those who have believed in Christ for salvation and made that statement of faith and began to walk in Him, all are welcome to read and learn how "The thief", (satan), comes only to steal and kill, and destroy. He is certainly as a fowler setting a snare for anyone of us, but Christ has come that all may have safety and life, and that all may have it more abundantly.

In every walk of life there are many extremely difficult trials and often a great deal of trouble, and let's face it, what life doesn't have trouble thrown into it from time to time? Some are trials from childhood and some are as adults, and many of these trials have been perpetrated against us by others. Some trials have been thrust upon us merely by a change of events, while other trials we have created for ourselves. One thing rings true in many trials. Either it will make us bitter or it will make us more like Christ, perfect and complete, lacking nothing.

> *My brethren, count it all joy when you fall into various trials, knowing that the testing of your faith produces patience. But let patience have its perfect work, that you may be perfect and complete, lacking nothing.*
>
> *James 1:2-4*

Bitterness can be a stealthy, under-cover emotion. Many times, those who are bitter in life for whatever reason, appear to be fine on the surface. They may attend church and possibly even work in the church. They may know lots of scripture, be able to direct someone in the ways of righteousness, carry a happy demeanor, and at face value even pleasant to be around. But spend some time with them and you will see they are not letting patience have its perfect work. They are not living the abundant life that Jesus desires for us. You will begin to see that something just doesn't add up with one who declares belief in the Great Physician. Why do I use this name here for Jesus, The Great Physician? I use it because one of the reasons He gave His life for us is so that we may be healed.

In ***Isaiah 53:5*** it says, ***"and by His stripes we are*** *healed."* While many believe that this statement reaches into the healing of disease and physical ailments, it most definitely means the healing of the effects of sin and the power it has over one's life. Sin kills and destroys life, but through Jesus Christ we can be healed from sin in our lives and blessed with a peaceful abundant life. As you are reading this, the Lord may be speaking to you. Light bulbs are coming on, or certain people are coming to mind. Maybe, just maybe, this describes you. If it does, don't fight it. Pray for God's guidance, strength, understanding, and healing as you read on.

Pursue peace with all people, and holiness, without which no one will see the Lord; looking carefully lest anyone fall short of the grace of God; lest any root of bitterness springing up cause trouble, and by this many become defiled. Hebrews 12:14-15

As we look at how one becomes bitter and the effects of bitterness in one's life, I hope to bring into clarity the even greater tragedy of bitterness in the life of a believer. We will first take a look at what bitterness in our life brings about. In the previous verse we see that bitterness in our life causes us to be defiled. Let's see what the scriptures tell us about "Being Defiled."

1

To the Pure All Things are Pure.

To the pure all things are pure, but to those who are defiled and unbelieving, nothing is pure.

Titus 1:15

In this verse Paul is addressing the issue of those who are forbidding others from eating certain foods or that it is sin to drink out of a dirty cup. He says, "to the pure all things are pure", meaning, to those who are pure in heart, to those who have been trained by God's word and by His pruning *John 15:1-2*, everything is ok to eat and nothing is to be refused. Dirty cup, clean cup, dirty dish, clean dish, there is no sin. Then he says, "But to those who are defiled and unbelieving nothing is pure". In this statement he is not talking about food anymore. He is saying that with the defiled and unbelieving, that because their heart is not pure in Christ by being trained by God's word and His pruning, that all that they think, feel, and do is tainted and in no way pure. For them, the defiled, nothing is pure.

The Greek word for "To the pure" is "Katharos" and it means, to be clean or pure. Physically, it means, purified by fire or in a similitude, like a vine cleansed by pruning and so fitted to bear fruit. In a Levitical sense it means, clean, the use of which is not forbidden, imparts no uncleanness. Ethically it means, free from corrupt desire, from sin and guilt. Free from every admixture of what is false. Sincere or genuine. Blameless or innocent. Unstained with the guilt of anything.

Who are the pure?

As we see from the Greek definition of the word Pure, it actually means, "one who has been purified by fire like a vine cleansed by pruning and so fitted to bear fruit. Strongs Concordance. We see an illustration of this in the gospel of John.

> *"I am the true vine, and My Father is the vinedresser. "Every branch in Me that does not bear fruit He takes away; and every branch that bears fruit He prunes, that it may bear more fruit. John 15:1-2*

When a believer bears fruit, the Lord prunes them that they may bear more fruit. This process of pruning is not always pleasant. It is actually cutting away unwanted parts of our character. These times of pruning usually are accompanied with a trial. It may be something someone has said or done to you that was mean and hateful. Or it may be a negative event that has happened in your life. While these things are done to you and or happening in your life, God's work of pruning you is to cut away your fleshly reaction to what has been done or said to you or the negative or difficult event that has come upon you. His goal is that you might bear the fruit of a godly response to what has happened to you. Allowing this process of God's pruning and our bearing more fruit is one facet in being pure. In this sense of being pure it also means that we respond properly to God's pruning of us and allow Him to cut away the actions and thought processes of our character that are in and of the flesh. Simply put, God's goal of the pruning process is for us to stop operating in the flesh and start operating in the Spirit. One who is pure responds positively to and receives the pruning of the Lord in their lives.

Ok, so check it out, I am not going to tell you that this is just a simple and easy thing to do. It's not. The process of how it works, or is supposed to work, is easy to explain, but there is no way we can get through this on our own. You must have a courageous trust in the living God that He will work this in you as He and you set forth to make changes in your life. Remember, our great Savior held His hand out to you and bid you to come and follow Him. The loving kindness with which God drew you to Him and caused you to see your need for the Savior, it is with that same love that our Father bids you to come now, in this sense, that you may bear more fruit and grow in Him. Every step of the way our loving Father is with us, filling us with His Spirit, strengthening us to overcome and allow Him to make the changes in our life that bring us closer and closer to Himself.

In another sense of the word. The pure are free from sin and guilt. They are blameless and innocent. This does not mean that they do not sin, because we all sin from time to time. It means that they do not practice sin. They practice righteousness. And when they sin, they repent quickly and keep walking with the Lord. When you walk this way in the Lord you are free from sin and guilt, you are blameless and innocent. You are pure.

In another sense of the word. The pure are free from every admixture of what is false. They are genuine and sincere. This means they are not fake or phony. What you see is what you get, whether they are in public or alone.

In a final sense of the word. The pure are unstained with the guilt of anything. We have already talked about being free from sin and guilt, but what about carrying around the guilt of things we have done. The pure believe, trust, and walk in the forgiveness of God. They are not uncaring about what they have done, but they trust in the forgiveness of God and do not carry around the guilt of past sins, mistakes, or bad decisions. As they do this, our loving Father heals their hearts in righteousness.

Who is clean?

We find an illustration of this in...

2 Timothy 2:19-21

> *"Nevertheless, the solid foundation of God stands, having this seal: "The Lord knows those who are His," and, "Let everyone who names the name of Christ depart from iniquity." But in a great house there are not only vessels of gold and silver, but also of wood and clay, some for honor and some for dishonor. Therefore if anyone cleanses himself from the latter, he will be a vessel for honor, sanctified and useful for the Master, prepared for every good work."*

So, we see that in departing from iniquity, which is repenting of sin, we go from being a vessel of dishonor which cannot be used, to a vessel of honor that has been cleansed, sanctified, and useful for the Master, prepared for every good work. One who is clean is repentant.

Free from corrupt desire.

> *"I beseech you therefore, brethren, by the mercies of God, that you present your bodies a living sacrifice, holy and acceptable to God, which is your reasonable service. And do not be conformed to this world, but be transformed by the renewing if*

your mind, that you may prove what is that good and acceptable and perfect will of God." Romans 12:1-2

In this verse the apostle Paul, in short, is begging the believers in Rome to read God's word, do exactly what it says that they may begin to have their minds renewed, desiring the things of God and not the things of the world, which are corrupt desires. Listen, it is true, we need to stop being conformed to this world. We need to crucify the flesh and stop walking in the corrupt desires of this world, but that should not be the main focus of the task. At the same time, we need also to be transformed by the renewing of our minds. So, yes, work on not sinning, and as you do, give even more attention to being transformed by the renewing your mind, Reading God's word and doing what it says! This will, so-to-speak, be killing two birds with one stone, with the focus on practicing righteousness. This is the way to become free from corrupt desire. Also, we see in **Galatians 5:24 "And those who are Christ's have crucified the flesh with its passions and desires." And in Luke 9:23 "Then He said to them all, "If anyone desires to come after Me, let him deny himself, and take up his cross daily, and follow Me."** Note: If anyone has the godly desire to come after Jesus, they must deny themselves. They must take up their cross daily, which means to die to the flesh, crucify your corrupt desires of the flesh daily. He then says, follow Me, which means to walk as He walked, follow His example, obey Him.

What is corrupt desire?

Matthew 15:17-20

> *"Do you not yet understand that whatever enters the mouth goes into the stomach and is eliminated? "But those things which proceed out of the mouth come from the heart, and they defile a man. "For out of the heart proceed evil thoughts, murders, adulteries, fornications, thefts, false witness, blasphemies. "These are the things which defile a man, but to eat with unwashed hands does not defile a man."*

1Corinthians 6:9-10

> *Do you not know that the unrighteous will not inherit the kingdom of God? Do not be deceived. Neither fornicators, nor idolaters, nor adulterers, nor homosexuals, nor sodomites, nor thieves, nor covetous, nor drunkards, nor revilers, nor extortioners will inherit the kingdom of God.*

Galatians 5:19-21

> *Now the works of the flesh are evident, which are: adultery, fornication, uncleanness, lewdness, idolatry, sorcery,*

> **hatred, contentions, jealousies, outbursts**
> **of wrath, selfish ambitions, dissensions,**
> **heresies, envy, murders, drunkenness,**
> **revelries, and the like; of which I tell you**
> **beforehand, just as I also told you in time**
> **past, that those who practice such things**
> **will not inherit the kingdom of God.**

I want you to notice that at the end of the list of the works of the flesh here in **Galatians 5:19-21** it has the phrase, "And the like." Paul here is not leaving anything to question with this statement in Galatians. He ends the list with, "And the like" so that the Galatians and all of us, will know that it is not just limited to this specific list of the works of the flesh stated here, but also anything that is even like these things are works of the flesh.

All that I have listed here in these verses, and the like, are corrupt desires.

All things are pure

To those who are pure in heart, they don't look at everything as though it were suspect. We might even call some of them, naïve. You may know a lot about the dark side of life, but because you have allowed the Lord to work in you and prune away the unwanted parts of your character, those thoughts of what you know, are not the first thing that your mind goes to. The word of God says, Love believes all things. This means that you believe the best out of every situation. This is the heart of, all things are pure. It certainly does not mean that even sin is pure in the eyes and thoughts of the pure, it just means that the best and most righteous thoughts are put forth in every situation until proven otherwise, and even then, the best thoughts are put forth in hoping for repentance in the individual or the betterment of the situation.

So, hopefully now, we have a pretty good picture of what it means to be pure and how the pure at heart look at things, in life. With this in mind, take some time to pray and seek the Lord on these things. Examine yourself to see if this is where the Lord has you currently or if He is speaking to you in that this is what He is wanting to build in your life. Perhaps you once had this heart and He is calling you back to renew this heart and strengthen these things in your life. Whatever the case, our God loves us and is always good toward us. Let Him have His way in you! It will only turn out to be your blessing and those around you!

2

But to Those Who are Defiled and Unbelieving

In the previous chapter we covered what it means to be pure and what the process of pruning entails. Now, we are coming to a place where some of the personal cost of not allowing the Lord to prune you is spelled out, the sin of bitterness. I would like to take this moment to say, any believer who gets to this place in their life, where they are truly bitter, was never forced down this road. If you are a believer in Jesus Christ, His Holy Spirit was convicting you all the way not to let this happen, but you would not allow God's pruning of your life in this area to take effect. Even at this moment, the choice is yours to turn from bitterness. Let's look at what the word defiled means.

The Greek word for Defiled is "Miaino" and means,
1. to dye with another color, to stain
2. to defile, pollute, sully, contaminate, soil
3. to defile with sins

In ***Hebrews 12:14-15*** we get a better look at how one can become defiled.

Pursue peace with all people, and holiness, without which no one will see the Lord; looking carefully lest anyone fall short of the grace of God; lest any root of bitterness springing up cause trouble, and by this many become defiled;

Here's how it works. When someone has done you wrong or you perceive that someone has done you wrong and you don't forgive that person and let It go, then you are not pursuing peace and holiness with all men. Keep in mind, this is part of the Lord's pruning, that you respond to these situations in the Spirit and not in the flesh. **Romans 12:18** says, ***"If it is possible, as much as depends on you, live peaceably with all men."*** The Greek word for peaceably is eireneuo (I-ray-new-o), and it means, to have peace, live peaceably, live in peace, and **to be at peace**. To be at peace with something or someone means that YOU are at peace with the situation or event. To be at peace within ourselves, with any wrong done to us, we must forgive the person or entity who wronged us. When you don't forgive and you continue with this heart of unforgiveness, you are not being careful to keep from falling short of the grace of God. A root of bitterness will spring up in you, and then you have become defiled, stained, sullied, or dyed with another color. Look at what the Lord says about sin, in Isaiah and Jeremiah.

*"Come now, and let us reason together,"
Says the LORD, "Though your sins are like
scarlet, they shall be as white as snow;
Though they are red like crimson, they
shall be as wool. Isaiah 1:18*

*Though you wash yourself with lye and use
much soap, the stain of your guilt is still
before Me, declares the Lord God. Jeremiah
2:22 (ESV translation)*

When we believed in Jesus for salvation, we came to
Him with our sins "like scarlet" and "red like crimson", but
through repentance and believing in Him He has made us
"white as snow". When we let bitterness into our lives we
become defiled and are stained again with sin. Do you see
how explicit the word of God is? It is awesome! Now, this
takes us back to what I said in the beginning, *"Bitterness
can be a stealthy, under-cover emotion. Many times, those
who are bitter in life for whatever reason, appear to be fine
on the surface. They may attend church and possibly even
work in the church. They may know lots of scripture, be
able to direct someone in the ways of righteousness, carry
a happy demeanor, and at face value even pleasant to be
around."* However, this is where the Lord sees the heart
and is able to say, 'I see the stain of your guilt.' We may
be able to hide this heart from some people, but not from
everyone, and we will certainly never be able to hide this
heart from God.

Now that we have a good overview of what it means to be defiled, let's take a look at what it means to be unbelieving.

The Greek word here for unbelieving is "Apistos" and it means...
1. unfaithful, faithless, (not to be trusted, perfidious)
2. incredible
    1. of things
3. unbelieving, incredulous
    1. without trust (in God)

The actual sentence from the Strongs concordance is...

"Of those among the Christians themselves who reject the true faith."

When the Word of God says, *"Pursue peace with all men and holiness, without which no one will see the Lord." Hebrews 12:14*, yet you harbor bitterness in your heart towards someone, you are rejecting the true faith and rejecting God's command. You are unbelieving that God's way is the only true way to live life and you are believing that your way is the right way. God's word is clear on the danger of living your life out your own way. We just read in Hebrews, without pursuing peace and holiness with all men, no one will see the Lord. And in *Proverbs 14:12* we see...

> *There is a way that seems right to a man,*
> *but its end is the way of death.*

All through God's word we see that "believe" and "obey" are synonymous. When we disobey God's word we are not believing. We see proof of this in **Hebrews 3:16-19**.

"For who, having heard, rebelled? Indeed, was it not all who came out of Egypt, led by Moses? Now with whom was He angry forty years? Was it not with those who sinned, whose corpses fell in the wilderness? And to whom did He swear that they would not enter His rest, but to those who did not obey? So, we see that they could not enter in because of unbelief."

John 3:16 "For God so loved the world that He gave His only begotten Son, that whoever believes in Him should not perish but have everlasting life.

Acts 5:32 "And we are His witnesses to these things and so also is the Holy Spirit whom God has given to those who obey Him."

Hebrews 5:9 "And having been perfected, He became the author of eternal salvation to all who obey Him."

> ***James 2:18-20** "But someone will say, "You have faith, and I have works." Show me your faith without your works, and I will show you my faith by my works. You believe that there is one God. You do well. Even the demons believe—and tremble! But do you want to know, O foolish man, that faith without works is dead?"*

Scripture is clear concerning what it means to believe. The believer in Jesus Christ has a certain look. His actions are different than those of the world. He is lead by the Spirit of God and His word, not his own way (flesh). It is through disobedience to God's word that we then allow a root of bitterness to spring up in us and by this become defiled, thus becoming stained again with sin and are not believing in Jesus. This is a wicked, wicked snare satan sets for us that plays right into the desires of our flesh.

3

Nothing is Pure

To those who are defiled and unbelieving **nothing is pure...**

Wow, that is heavy statement.

Paul, in this portion of scripture is no longer talking about food. What he is addressing is the fact that once you get to the place where you are defiled and unbelieving you don't see anything pure. Everything you think, see, feel, and understand is tainted with sin. He goes on to say, **"Even their mind and conscience are defiled."** In the mind is where all the work of understanding, determining, feeling, judging and perceiving is done. So, when the mind is defiled (Stained with sin), all of the perceiving and understanding, the feeling, judging and determining, are all tainted and impure.

The conscience is the soul, making the distinction between what is morally good and bad prompting us to choose the good and shun the bad. So, when your conscience is defiled (Stained with sin), not only is your distinction between what is morally right and wrong tainted and impure, but the prompting to choose the good and shun the bad is tainted and impure as well. If this sounds familiar to you, it should. It is the picture of our "old man" or "woman". It is who we used to be before we were saved by Jesus and were filled with His Holy Spirit. At that time, we were led by our own flesh according to the world. We were truly dead in our sin. Once we believed in Jesus though, He made all things new and gave us a spirit of a sound mind. ***2 Timothy 1:7, "For God has not given us a spirit of fear, but of power and of love and of a sound mind."*** However, when you allow a root of bitterness to spring up in you, you move from having that sound mind to now having a defiled (Stained with sin) mind. This does not mean that the day we receive Christ we are perfect in all things and are perfectly obedient to the Lord in every way. What this means is that each of us upon receiving Jesus have been given the spirit of a sound mind in that now we have the capability, through the Spirit, to understand the things of God and the capability to choose those things as good for us over the things and the ways of the world and our flesh which are not good for us. To put a finer tip on it, the word of God says,

> ***But the natural man does not receive the things of the Spirit of God, for they are foolishness to him; nor can he know them, because they are spiritually discerned. 1Corinthians 2:14***

Having said these last things, I would like to take this time to ask if there is anyone one who is reading this and not understanding what is actually being said. If you have not received Christ as your Lord and Savior that is one reason why you may not be understanding what is being said here. I would like to give you the opportunity right now to receive Jesus Christ as your Lord and Savior. It was in a book that was given to me to read that I came to Jesus. It wasn't at an alter in a church or even an outreach event. It was in my living room on my couch. The scriptures say that we are all born into sin and condemned to hell. **Romans 5:12-19** It also says that the wages of sin are death. **Romans 6:23** This means that there must be payment for my sin, meaning that every individual must make restitution for their sin by dying for it and spending eternity in hell in the Lake of Fire. God, not wanting anyone to die and go to hell, sent His Son Jesus Christ to die and pay the penalty for sin one time for all and then He raise Him to life again on the third day. If you will believe in Jesus and what He has done by dying in your place on the cross, then your debt for sin is paid by Jesus in full and you are saved and you are NOT condemned to hell, but will be with Jesus and the rest of the believers in heaven on the last day forever and ever.

If you would like to receive Jesus as your Lord and Savior, here is a prayer that you can pray to receive Him. If you pray this prayer and mean it in your heart then you will be saved from the condemnation of hell and be on your way to see the amazing love that God has for you!

Father, please forgive me for all my sins. I thank You for Your forgiveness. I receive Your Son Jesus as my Lord and Savior. Please fill me with Your Holy Spirit and please give me strength to live for You and not the things of this world. Thank You for sending Your Son to die for my sin and I thank You for loving me. Please lead me and guide me in every way. In Jesus' name. Amen.

If you prayed that prayer, you are saved!!! Now, walk with the Lord. Get a Bible and read it and do what it says. Find a Bible teaching church and attend! You will find more concerning this step you have just made at the end of this book under, Salvation. Now, let's carry on...

They profess to know God, but in works they deny Him.

There are countless people throughout the world who say that they know God. Some are truly talking about Yahweh, the only true God, however, they do not really know Him, and they choose to deal with Him on their terms. I have spoken with many people over the years about their walk and relationship with God. Many times, one of the questions I ask is, "Where will you go when you die?" The standard answer is, "Well, I hope heaven." Another question I ask is, "Do you read your Bible?" The standard answer is, "Not as much as I should." Both of these questions should have a clear and decisive answer from one who knows God; I am going to heaven to be with my Savior Jesus, and Yes, I'm in the word constantly. The problem is, many people are willing to take all of God's promises of love and good fortune and protection from Him but not walk as He has called us to walk. They are more than willing to partake in all the goodness and loving kindness and the hope of heaven one day that comes through faith in Jesus Christ, but they are not willing to **Fight the good fight of faith! 1Timothy 6:12.** Nor are they willing **to Be doers of the word and not hearers only, deceiving themselves James 1:22**. They are not willing to **Trust in the Lord with all their heart and lean not on their own understanding and in all their ways acknowledge Him so that He may direct their paths Proverbs 3:5-6**. They are not willing to **Put off the old man with his deeds and put on the new man who is renewed in knowledge according to the image of Him who created him. Colossians 3:9-10** Nor are they willing to **Crucify the flesh with its passions and desires. Galatians 5:24** They are not willing to stop living life their way and live it God's way. They are not willing to repent, to forgive, or to love. We find in the church today that there is a horrible witness of what biblical truth looks like lived out, which stems from an equally horrible illiteracy in biblical knowledge. Many are willing to hear the call to receive Jesus as their Savior and reap the benefits of divine protection, all the blessings, even the hope of heaven, but they are not willing to follow Jesus. Many believers do not read their bible so they really do not know who God is and what an amazingly rich life He desires for each of us. This leads to more trouble in that they just live according to who they think God is, and since they are human their thoughts of who God is are humanistic.

James gives us a clear picture of what must take place in the life of one who says they believe in Jesus, one who says they know God.

James 2:14-26

What does it profit, my brethren, if someone says he has faith but does not have works? Can faith save him? If a brother or sister is naked and destitute of daily food, and one of you says to them, "Depart in peace, be warmed and filled," but you do not give them the things which are needed for the body, what does it profit? Thus also faith by itself, if it does not have works, is dead. But someone will say, "You have faith, and I have works." Show me your faith without your works, and I will show you my faith by my works. You believe that there is one God. You do well. Even the demons believe—and tremble! But do you want to know, O foolish man, that faith without works is dead?

Was not Abraham our father justified by works when he offered Isaac his son on the altar? Do you see that faith was working together with his works, and by works faith was made perfect? And the Scripture was fulfilled which says, "Abraham believed God, and it was accounted to him for righteousness." And he was called the friend of God. You see then that a man is justified by works, and not by faith only. Likewise, was not Rahab the harlot also justified by works when she received the messengers and sent them out another way? For as the body without the spirit is dead, so faith without works is dead also.

Also, in *Ephesians 2:10*

For we are His workmanship, created in Christ Jesus for good works, which God prepared before-hand that we should walk in them.

And also, *Titus 3:14*

And let our people also learn to maintain good works, to meet urgent needs, that they may not be unfruitful.

So, those who have become defiled through bitterness profess to know God, but because they won't forgive and love one another and they won't submit to the pruning of God to build their character into what He wants, in these very works they deny Him.

Being abominable, disobedient, and disqualified for every good work. Titus 1:16

Abominable means to be detestable, a sense of disgust and loathing. It means something that is deserving intense dislike. **This is not a place you want to be in, with God.** Disobedient means exactly what it says, they disobey God. We have already read how the children of Israel couldn't enter God's rest because of disobedience, *Hebrews 3:18-19* **(Again, not a good place to be in, with the Lord)**, and we have read how believe and obey are synonymous.

Disqualified for every good work is an interesting statement. We see people in places of church authority, people in places of ministry, we even read about the Pharisees, Sadducees, the Chief Priests, and all the religious leaders of the biblical times who were serving in places of a good work, but have missed the mark because of sin in their lives. So, if we see these people in places of authority in ministry who are clearly disqualified for every good work, why are they in these places of serving God and the church? Some have entered that good work when their hearts were soft and humble. They shunned evil and walked in what is good before the Lord, but somewhere along the way they let sin of some sort and or bitterness creep into their lives and distort the idea and vision that the Lord had for that good work. King Saul was one who started out well and unfortunately ended badly.

1Samuel 15:17

> **When you were little in your own eyes, were you not head of the tribes of Israel? And did not the Lord anoint you king over Israel? Now the Lord sent you on a mission, and said, 'Go, and utterly destroy the sinners, the Amalekites, and fight against them until they are consumed.' "Why then did you not obey the voice of the Lord? Why did you swoop down on the spoil, and do evil in the sight of the Lord?"**

Here we see pride in Saul's life disqualifying him from the good work of being king over Israel. When we understand that we need to be "little", meaning humble, in everything, and that the Lord allows us to serve Him in **HIS PLAN** for our life, that is being humble and that is when we are qualified for the good work that God has for us. When we think that we have a better idea or a better plan than God or that we can tweak His plan and make it a little better like Saul thought, or when we think that we don't need to forgive and love people even though God said to, that is when we have become "BIG" in our own eyes, prideful. That is when we have put our thoughts and desires above the Lord and have become disqualified by our own actions.

Keep this in mind also, the word says, ***"Some men's sins are clearly evident preceding them to judgment, but those of some men follow later. 1Timothy 5:24*** Sometimes we can see the sin in people's lives right away, but sometimes people are very good at hiding it for quite some time, if they are even aware and not completely deceived. This is also why Paul gives the command to Timothy to **lay hands on no man hastily 1Timothy 5:22**. Appointing people to good works in the church should be done carefully and methodically so that the individual's godly character and gifting or lack thereof may be brought to light first before the committed appointment. Another thing to realize is that man may appoint people to a good work that God never would. Just because you see someone in a position of a good work in the church does not mean that God put them there. It may not even mean that they were called to such a position. Nonetheless, when you are defiled because of bitterness in your life you are disqualified for every good work.

Well, in the midst of explaining how this terrible sin of bitterness defiles us completely, even down to the mind and conscience, I hope that if you were not a believer in Jesus before you started reading this book, you are now! Although sin and the workings of it must be spelled out so that the wise may escape the snare of the devil, the mighty hand and heart of God is always sure to bring the saving message of the gospel. If you have prayed that prayer from earlier in this chapter there is great reason to shout for joy, for you have passed from death into life.

4

The Secret Agent (Pride)

Somewhat like you would find in a murder mystery where all the characters are brought in one by one as the story unfolds, we find it is the least suspected character in the whole story who turns out to be the secret agent, and I guess that's why they are called a, secret agent. Well, just as in these novels, pride is one of those characters that plays a big part in bitterness, but often isn't revealed to its beholder until sometime later.

I once spoke with a person who had such hostility towards a church they used to attend that it was majorly notable. In speaking with them, I found out they had been involved working in the background ministry of the church. They had seen things that they described as nothing less than hypocrisy. Now it had been some years since this person had any dealings with this church, but the bitterness in their heart over these things made it as though it had just happened yesterday. One thing that was clearly evident was that this person had no compassion for the people at this church, only judgment.

This person's heart was so black with bitterness that they were completely blinded to the fact that they themselves were capable of falling in the very same manner, and had indeed fallen from grace, just in a different manner, through bitterness. One of the most clever lies from satan is that we feel we are justified in our position of bitterness and unforgiveness because we have been wronged. It sounds right. On paper it looks right. But in truth it is the exact opposite of what God says is good and right.

Whenever you can hold your heart steady against your brother or sister with such disdain and disgust over sin in their lives, your heart is so thick with ungodly judgment and pride that you are in as much trouble if not more than they are. The word of God tells us in *Matthew 7:1-5*

"Judge not, that you be not judged. "For with what judgment you judge, you will be judged; and with the measure you use, it will be measured back to you. "And why do you look at the speck in your brother's eye, but do not consider the plank in your own eye? "Or how can you say to your brother, 'Let me remove the speck from your eye'; and look, a plank is in your own eye? "Hypocrite! First remove the plank from your own eye, and then you will see clearly to remove the speck from your brother's eye.

In this section of scripture Jesus is teaching us the correct way for judging sin in someone's life, and while we are not going to get in to the actual application of this part of scripture, I would like to pull something from it. In the simplest terms, Jesus says, when you are going to judge a matter concerning someone and sin in their life, first make sure that there is no sin in your life. You see, the other person may very well have sin in their life, but if you have sin in your life, you will never be able to see clearly concerning the sin in anyone else's life. You will not be thinking or speaking from a place of righteousness. It is a prideful thing to approach or look at someone in judgement concerning their sin when you can't see or refuse to repent of your own sin.

God's word tells us in **Galatians 6:1**

> **Brethren, if a man is overtaken in any trespass, you who are spiritual restore such a one in a spirit of gentleness, considering yourself lest you also be tempted.**

This verse is a powerhouse of information! **If anyone is overtaken in any trespass**; This is what we are talking about, right? Someone has done something wrong to you or you see that they are in sin of some sort. The first criteria stated here is, if you are going to say something about it, you must be spiritual. So, what does that mean? Well, the Greek word for spiritual here is **pneu ma ti kos**, and it means, "to be as part of the man which is akin to God and serves as His instrument or organ". Have you heard the term, next of kin? That means your closest family by blood. To be akin to God means that you belong to Him and move and speak by His Holy Spirit. Next, the verse says to **Restore that person in a spirit of gentleness**. That word Restore in Greek is **ka tar te zo**, and it means to mend (what has been broken or rent), to repair. It could be understood as, setting a broken bone. In any case it means to bring healing, to restore to the way it should be, unbroken. Next, it says to do this in a spirit of gentleness considering yourself lest you also be tempted. This means just what it says. Speak to them, approach them with all gentleness, having a mind and a heart of humility, understanding that it could very well be you committing that same sin. If you think for one moment that you are justified in pointing the finger at people who are in sin or have committed sin against you, with disgust and disdain, whether you know it or not, pride has taken residence in your heart and has aided the process of bringing you to a place of horrible bitterness.

What I am wanting you to take away from this is that, in life, people make horrible errors in judgment and hurt others deeply. People sometimes say and do things out of anger, frustration, jealousy, bitter envy, and sometimes on purpose. Sometimes people sin against others, AND YOU AND I DO TOO.

I want to be sure to give grace to you, my brother's and sister's. The initial response to sin perpetrated directly against you could be a little crazy. I know early in my walk with God, when someone had done me wrong, they would certainly be judged harshly and without any thought to the fact that I could have done the same thing and worse to others. However, as I continued to walk with God, He continued to reveal more of who I really was. Yes, you read that correctly. He revealed to me who I really was. I am one of those people who have done and said horrible mean things to others and have needed forgiveness and restoration. And honestly, it is something I need to be mindful of, being swift to hear and slow to speak. It is from this vantage point, knowing and remembering who I really was, that I can lavishly forgive and have grace for others.

Finally, the word of God says in **Hebrews 5:1-2**

> *For every high priest taken from among men is appointed for men in things pertaining to God, that he may offer both gifts and sacrifices for sins. He can have compassion on those who are ignorant and going astray, since he himself is also subject to weakness. Because of this he is also required as for the people, so also for himself, to offer sacrifices for sins. And no man takes this honor to himself, but he who is called by God, just as Arron was.*

I find it quite interesting that the one who has been

appointed high priest, I mean the very guy who must have a walk so close to God that God Himself would appoint him in the duty of high priest to offer the sacrifices for the sin of the people, must offer sacrifices for his own sin first. Listen, please, no one is above another. Not the high priest, not your pastor, and guess what, not you or I, either. Every person is susceptible to sin, especially if we are not watchful. Pride causes me to put myself on a level much higher than everyone else when it comes to sin. Plenty of mercy and compassion for myself, but none for all others. Pride causes me to see those who fall into sin as less than myself, not as smart as I am, and certainly not worthy of any compassion or grace as I would be. God's word says, ***"Let him who thinks he stands, take heed lest he fall". 1Corinthians 10:12 and also, "For if anyone thinks himself to be something, when he is nothing, he deceives himself." Galatians 6:3***

In conclusion, I spoke of pride as being a, secret agent. A secret agent, many times is put in place, whether it's a good agent or an evil agent, so that they may help put things in play for a certain outcome. In this instance you may think that you are completely justified in the way that you think and feel about a person or a situation, and the person or situation may very well be in the wrong, HOWEVER, it is that underlying thread of pride, that you don't think you have, that (secret agent), that you have allowed in to help satan put things in play in your life for his (satan's) outcome. Remember,

"The thief does not come except to steal, and to kill, and to destroy. I have come that they may have life, and that they may have it more abundantly. John 10:10

Yes, Steal, Kill, and Destroy, that is satan's plan and desired outcome for you.

5

What Now?

I could say that repentance is what is needed now, but if it were that simple you probably would have done that already. And, while repentance is something that definitely needs to happen, I believe that only a change of perspective and heart will bring about repentance. Why do I say this when clearly the bible teaches that repentance comes through the conviction of the Holy Spirit? I say this because when bitterness sets in you have already ignored the Holy Spirit on a couple different levels. Don't take what I am saying wrong. A change of perspective and heart concerning sin also comes from the Holy Spirit, and I am hoping to convince you to listen to Him and repent. With that being said, let's look at God's perspective towards us.

All sin is against God. It doesn't matter who did what to whom or why it was done or when it was done. All sin is directly against God. This is because the term 'sin' means to miss the mark. Well, neither you nor I have set that mark. The mark was set by God. When you go past the mark you have missed it, and therefore have sinned against Him. So, what does God do? Does He just forget those who sin against Him? What is God's heart in this matter? Let's look in **Romans 5:6-8**.

> *For when we were still without strength, in due time Christ died for the ungodly. For scarcely for a righteous man will one die; yet perhaps for a good man someone would even dare to die. But God demonstrates His own love toward us, in that while we were still sinners, Christ died for us.*

God's heart is always for restoration! He knows that mankind will always fall short and sin against Him, and His heart is always to draw them out of sin and into righteousness. This includes you as well. Scripture tells us that **all have sinned and fall short of the glory of God. Romans 3:23**. Scripture also tells us in **1John 1:8-10**

> *If we say that we have no sin, we deceive ourselves, and the truth is not in us. If we confess our sins, He is faithful and just to forgive us our sins and to cleans us from all unrighteousness. If we say that we have not sinned, we make Him a liar, and His word is not in us.*

If you look at these verses here in 1John, it points out

clearly that we have sin to deal with in our lives, every single one of us, but right in the middle is a beautiful statement of the heart of God towards us.

> **If we confess our sins, He is faithful and just to forgive us our sins and to cleans us from all unrighteousness. 1John 1:9**

Do you remember in ***John 8:1-11*** the story of the woman who was caught in the act of adultery? She was brought before Jesus by the scribes and the Pharisees, accused of being caught in the very act of adultery. They said to Jesus, 'the law states that she should be stoned, but what do You say?' Jesus stoops down on the ground and begins writing on the ground with His finger, as though He does not hear them at all. As they continued asking Him, He stands up and says to them, "He who is without sin among you, let him throw a stone at her first." Then He stooped down again and wrote on the ground. Now, keep this in mind, the scripture does not say that she was innocent of committing adultery. We can pretty much conclude that she was not innocent by Jesus' words, "Go and sin no more. I want to point out that her sin was directly against Jesus, and even the scribes and Pharisees, being convicted by Jesus' statement, "whoever of you who is without sin, throw a stone at her first." leave one by one until it is only Jesus and the woman left. Jesus says to her, "Woman, where are those accusers of yours? Has no one condemned you?" She said, "No one, Lord." And Jesus said to her, "Neither do I condemn you; go and sin no more."

41

I want you to put yourself in the woman's place for a moment. Oh wait, you've been in the woman's place before and so have I. It may not have been adultery, but it was some kind of sin. Maybe it was fornication or drunkenness. Maybe it was lying or stealing or both. Maybe it was extortion or pride or causing division. Whatever it was it was something, and you and I were both in desperate need of forgiveness and will be again in the future. Listen, the heart of God is that no one would perish, that no one would see an eternal death.

> *"Say to them: 'As I live,' says the Lord God, 'I have no pleasure in the death of the wicked, but that the wicked turn from his way and live. Turn, turn from your evil ways! For why should you die, O house of Israel?' Ezekiel 33:11*

> *The Lord is not slack concerning His promise, as some count slackness, but is longsuffering toward us, not willing that any should perish but that all should come to repentance. 2Peter 3:9*

> *For this is good and acceptable in the sight of God our Savior, who desires all men to be saved and to come to the knowledge of the truth. 1Timothy 2:3-4*

The heart of God is that the wicked would not die but that they would turn from their wickedness and be saved. The heart of God is that all men would be saved and come to the knowledge of the truth. The heart of God is to be longsuffering, waiting for men to come to repentance so that they would not perish. Is this your heart, that none would perish or is your heart only concerned that you won't perish? I have heard it said, "O how horrible does our sin look when someone else is committing it." Why is that? Why is our sin much more acceptable and much more deserving of grace and patience and understanding when I am committing it? If someone else is committing that same sin, especially against us, there is no mercy? We require them to pay to the fullest. Do we not see ourselves? Do we really not see that we are no different than all of mankind who must deal with the law of sin??? **Romans 7:25** Do we really not see that we ourselves, are given great patience from the Lord as we work through our own life and sin?

When someone sins against you, do you forgive them? Do you love them as you love yourself? Do you have compassion for them in that they have sinned, just as you have sinned at times?

6

The Same Sufferings

Do you remember in *Ephesians 6:10-13* when it is speaking about putting on the armor of God? It starts out talking about putting on the armor that you may be able to stand against the wiles or methods of the devil, but then it says something very interesting. It says that we do not wrestle against flesh and blood. Let's stop right there. What does this mean? It means that my fight is not with my spouse. It is not with the guy that just cut me off on the freeway. It is not with the boss or co-worker who makes every day a nightmare at work, but my fight is with the powers and forces of darkness and wickedness that come against me.

> *For we do not wrestle against flesh and blood, but against principalities, against powers, against the rulers of the darkness of this age, against spiritual hosts of wickedness in the heavenly places. Ephesians 6:12*

You see, when Paul said in **Romans 7:18, "In me, that is in my flesh, nothing good dwells",** his assessment of the flesh was correct. There is nothing good about the flesh at all. The flesh is the part of me that can and will submit to these influences of darkness, and follow their temptation into sin, **If I allow it.** These hosts of evil works want to move me in the flesh to hate, despise, and be bitter toward others. Once I really grasp and understand what the scripture says here, that my fight is with these evil powers of darkness and not with people, then I am free to forgive and love, even my enemies.

Let's build on this a little more. Do you remember in **1Peter 5:9** where it says that the same sufferings are experienced by your brotherhood in the world? And also, in **1 Corinthians 10:13** it says, **"No temptation has overtaken you except such as is common to man."** Being tempted to sin is certainly a suffering that all of those who believe in Jesus Christ experience. Daily, we have to fight the good fight of faith and not succumb to temptation. And furthermore, it is the same temptations that are common to all men. There is nothing new under the sun in anyone's life when it comes to temptation. We may be tempted in different things according to each one's desires, mine in this way and yours in that way, but there are millions of others tempted the exact same way you are and the same for me.

In life we have those who are practiced at crucifying the flesh and through Christ have become pretty good at it. Then we have those who aren't too good at it and really don't put much effort into allowing the Lord to perfect this in their life. We also have those who haven't been saved very long and may be trying but still have a way to go. Then we have those who are not saved at all and their only control may be whatever morals they were raised with. Whatever it is, we must be able to look upon people and realize that they are under the same fire from the powers of darkness that we are and that we don't always do well at resisting the powers of darkness either.

What About the Willing?

Oh sure, there are people who are willingly following after the flesh with hearts that are as black as the night, but that should never stop you or I from seeing passed what they are doing to the truth, and the truth is, they do not know what they are doing. If they really knew what the truth is and the end of all those who practice evil, they would stop today and believe in Jesus. However, the god of this age has blinded their minds. *2Corinthians 4:3-4* Jesus, on the cross said,

> *"Father forgive them, for they know not what they do." Luke 23:34* And Stephen says in *Acts 7:60* as he was being stoned? *"Lord, do not charge them with this sin."*

Using Wisdom

I think that it is only wise since we are talking about dealing with people in our lives that may be causing heartache and trouble, to state clearly what I am not saying. While the Scriptures teach us such things as, ***Romans 15:1, 'We then who are strong ought to bear with the scruples of the weak, and not to please ourselves.'*** And ***1Corinthians 13:4-7, Love suffers long and is kind***. And ***Galatians 5:22, 'But the fruit of the Spirit is love... Long-suffering.'*** I believe it is equally as important that you do not leave yourself vulnerable in any way to someone who would harm you or take advantage of you, for the Scriptures also say in ***Philippians 2:4, 'Let each of you look out not only for your own interest, but also for the interest of others.'*** This verse is telling us that it is ok to look out for our own interest, but at the same time also looking out for others. You should be discerning and watchful. You do not have to stay in every situation or continue to keep company with those you cannot trust. I know a man who, at his job, was being taken advantage of. He would tell me that when he started the job it was for one area of work. Then he watched as people would quit and their job task would be moved over to him. Of course, there was no increase in pay for the extra work. This would go on to happen a couple of times. It really weighed heavily on him as his work load was crazy. One day he said to me, he sees God using this job to work things out of his character that shouldn't be there. Again, be discerning and prayerful. God may want you to stay where you are to use that situation to build your character. Or, He may say, 'Remove yourself from that situation.' In ***1Corinthians 5:9-13 Paul says not to keep company with anyone named a brother who is in sexual sin. 1Corinthians 15:33*** says, ***"Do not be deceived, evil company corrupts good habits."*** In ***2Thessalonians 3:14*** it says, ***"And if anyone does not obey our word in this epistle, note that person and do not keep company with him, that he may be ashamed."*** In all things, be wise.

Love people as you love yourself.

Close your eyes and tell me the second greatest commandment. Do you know it? Do you know it by heart?

> ***And the second, is like it: 'You shall love your neighbor as yourself.' Matthew 22:39***

Ok, just think for a minute. What if you are that person who has just handled a situation completely wrong with someone? What if it is you who has horribly hurt someone? Maybe you blew up on them and chewed them out all over a misunderstanding. If your first thought is, I wouldn't do that, you probably are going to need a different book... lol. No seriously. Listen, I don't care how close to the Lord you are or think you are, you are capable of sin and you do sin. Now, back to the question. What if it is you that has made a huge mistake and sinned against someone? HOW WOULD YOU WANT THEM TO RESPOND? Would you want them to react with utter disdain and bitter hatred toward you, not forgiving and not having any grace or mercy on you at all? How about instead, someone responding with forgiveness and mercy, giving you grace (favor) as one who is subject to the same temptations as you are, being an equal part of this fallen creation with the same tendencies to think of self over others? Unfortunately, all too often, the first example is how people react. They forget the second greatest commandment, "You shall love your neighbor as yourself." If you truly love your neighbor as yourself you will respond the way you would like to be treated. The question was, how do you want people to respond to you when you make a horrible mistake, when you sin against them. You want them to respond with love, giving you the benefit of the doubt. You want them to respond with forgiveness, gentleness, grace (favor), mercy, and a heart to restore the relationship. If this is how you love yourself, if this is the standard that you set for how you treat yourself, then you must love all others this way. Also, it is a command from God and not a suggestion. As a matter of fact, Jesus said, "On these two commandments hang all the law and the prophets. *Matthew 22:36-40.* This means that the law He sent to reveal our sin to us and all the prophets that He has sent and still sends warning the people to repent and turn back to Him, were done by God to get us to this one place where we would love God with all our heart, soul, mind, and strength and love our neighbor as ourselves.

As we see here, the same sufferings of man are not

limited to just the hardships that come against us, but we all share in the same sufferings of spiritual growth and crucifying the flesh. With this in mind, what is your heart in the matter? When you see someone in sin or even sinning against you, do you love them? Do you have compassion on them, realizing that they may be losing ground in our common fight against the flesh? Do you seek to restore them or do you condemn them and cast them aside?

7

Forgiveness

Wow, so this is a hot subject! Don't put the book down! I have talked with people over the years that expressed to me the difficulty they have had in forgiving people. Sometimes people can't get passed what someone else has done or said to them no matter how small or how great the offence was. As we venture off here into the scriptures concerning forgiveness, I do not want you to get the idea that I am making light of certain situations you may be in or things that have happened to you personally. Surely there are things and offences that have happened to us that while we need to forgive the offenders, it will take a great deal more of allowing the Lord to heal our hearts to get to that place of forgiveness. May I say to those of this sort, the Lord knows how deep your pain is and is patient and kind and faithful to walk you along through this process, if you allow Him. We will go in depth concerning God's healing in chapter 8.

Let us press on! There is a parable that Jesus tells us about forgiveness that is clear cut and straight to the point. In ***Matthew 18:21-35*** it says...

> ***Then Peter came to Him and said, "Lord, how often shall my brother sin against me, and I forgive him? Up to seven times?" Jesus said to him, "I do not say to you, up to seven times, but up to seventy times seven. "Therefore the kingdom of heaven is like a certain king who wanted to settle accounts with his servants. "And when he had begun to settle accounts, one was brought to him who owed him ten thousand talents.***
>
> ***"But as he was not able to pay, his master commanded that he be sold, with his wife and children and all that he had, and that payment be made. "The servant therefore fell down before him, saying, 'Master, have patience with me, and I will pay you all.' "Then the master of that servant was moved with compassion, released him, and forgave him the debt. "But that servant went out and found one of his fellow servants who owed him a hundred denarii; and he laid hands on him and took him by the throat, saying,***

'Pay me what you owe!' "So his fellow servant fell down at his feet and begged him, saying, 'Have patience with me, and I will pay you all.' "And he would not, but went and threw him into prison till he should pay the debt.

"So when his fellow servants saw what had been done, they were very grieved, and came and told their master all that had been done. "Then his master, after he had called him, said to him, 'You wicked servant! I forgave you all that debt because you begged me. 'Should you not also have had compassion on your fellow servant, just as I had pity on you?' "And his master was angry, and delivered him to the torturers until he should pay all that was due to him. "So My heavenly Father also will do to you if each of you, from his heart, does not forgive his brother his trespasses.

So, how do I follow that up? Well, let's go back over it and break it down, although the scripture is pretty straight forward here. Peter asks the Lord, "How often shall my brother sin against me and I forgive him? Up to seven times?" Jesus gives His answer to forgive seventy times seven and then digs right into the parable of how the king forgave the debt of his servant, but very quickly the servant forgot what had been done for him. He therefore treated his fellow servant quite different than the king treated him and had no compassion or pity on him at all. Why do you suppose this was? The servant to the king was forgiven a great debt, but he didn't really appreciate the depth of what had been done for him. I believe that is the key. Scripture talks about giving the sacrifice of thanksgiving to God. ***Psalm 116:17 Hebrews 13:15***. Thankfulness creates a depth of wisdom and compassion. A thankful heart is not quickly made bitter. Had the king's servant taken a moment to sit and think about what had just been done for him and responded, not with just a 'Thank you', but with thanksgiving, really acknowledging what had just been done for him, the outcome of how he treated his fellow servant may have been much different. Let me ask you, when was the last time you thanked God for your salvation? When was the last time you thanked God for all that He has delivered you from? As I said, a thankful heart creates a depth of wisdom and compassion, because as I remember what God has done in my own life by giving Him continual thanks, He reveals a greater depth of His love for me. He shows me the patience that He has for me while He is working things (sin) out of my life. He shows me how far off the mark I really am and then lovingly leads me back. How far off the mark are you? These next few verses are filled with the Father's love for us, starting with the

23 Psalm.

The Lord is my Shepherd; I shall not want.
He makes me to lie down in green pastures;
He leads me beside the still waters.
He restores my soul; He leads me in the paths
Of righteousness for His names sake.
Yea, though I walk through the valley of the shadow
Of death, I will fear no evil; for you are with me; Your rod
and Your staff they comfort me.
You prepare a table before me in the
Presence of my enemies;
You anoint my head with oil; My cup runs over.
Surely goodness and mercy shall follow me all the days
of my life;
And I will dwell in the house of the Lord forever.

And **Hosea 11:4** The Lord speaking of Ephraim,
I drew them with gentle cords,
With bands of love,
And I was to them as those who take the yoke from their
neck.
I stooped and fed them.

And **Matthew 11:28-30**
"Come to Me, all you who labor and are heavy laden, and I
will give you rest. "Take My yoke upon you and learn from
Me, for I am gentle and lowly in heart, and you will find rest
for your souls. "For My yoke is easy and My burden is light."

And ***Psalm 103:2-12***

Bless the Lord, O my soul; and forget not all of His benefits:
Who forgives all your iniquities,
Who heals all your diseases, who redeems your life
From destruction,
Who crowns you with lovingkindness and tender mercies,
Who satisfies your mouth with good things,
So that your youth is renewed like the eagle's.
The Lord executes righteousness and justice for all who
Are oppressed.
He made known His ways to Moses, His acts to the children
Of Israel.
The Lord is merciful and gracious, slow to anger, and
Abounding in mercy.
He will not always strive with us, nor will he keep His
Anger forever.
He has not dealt with us according to our sins, nor
punished us according to our iniquities.
For as the heavens are high above the earth, so
Great is His mercy toward those who fear Him;
As far as the east is from the west,
So far has He removed our transgressions from us.

If the Lord treats me with such love and mercy after all the sin I have committed against Him, how could I ever treat someone any different when they sin against me? These are just a few verses of God's love for us. The bible is packed full of God's message of love and forgiveness for us from cover to cover. Have you not seen, have you not heard, have you not experienced in your very own life the loving kindness of the Lord toward you and all who will call upon Him? Surely you can look back at your life and see the wonder of God at work forgiving your sin when you repent, healing your wounds from sin in your life, being patient with you while you struggled with sin and flesh. Can you recall it? Do you remember those times? Noting these things in life and living a thankful life to God will create a heart that forgives with compassion. Bitterness in the heart will make you blind to all of these things. It will make you blind to the amazing wonders that God has and is waiting to accomplish in your life. You will not see when good comes, because your focus is on you and on you alone.

Dear saint, have you missed the mark? Are you unforgiving? Are there limits to your forgiveness as Peter may have thought when he asked Jesus, *'How often shall my brother sin against me and I forgive him? Up to seven times?' Matthew 18:21* Do you draw a line with people concerning forgiveness, maybe your spouse, friend, or a boss? Have you ever thought or said the words, "That's it! I'm not forgiving you anymore. You keep doing this over and over again." Might I suggest, that is more of a situation of how you are dealing with the persons behavior and what you are allowing into your life, rather than you being able to forgive them. For instance, I can forgive you for taking advantage of me. I can even do that a couple of times, but at some point, wisdom would say to remove myself from that place where you are able to take advantage of me.

But what about things that you can't control? Maybe a person lying to you? Maybe it is a family member. It may not be someone you can just stop dealing with. It might be a co-worker or your teenager. The bottom line is, you must forgive.

Back to the parable in **Matthew 18** where we see a king moved with compassion to forgive the debt of his servant. The master didn't just give him more time to pay, he forgave the debt. The servant no longer owed the ten thousand talents. Listen, Peter, along with all of us, you and I, came into this world with a sin debt that we could never afford to pay. Who knows what this king was thinking. The scriptures say he was moved with compassion. Maybe he thought, this man has a wife and kids to support, there's no way he will be able to pay off this debt and have a full fruitful life with his family. The scriptures only say he was moved with compassion and forgave the debt. God is moved with compassion when He sees us having come into this world with a sin debt so huge that we will never be able to pay it. I want you to note that the ten thousand talents had to come from somewhere. Even though the king forgave the debt and the servant didn't have to pay it back, someone had to pay that debt. The king payed it himself. It was his own loss of money. Do you know that is exactly what God has done for us by sending Jesus to pay our sin debt? God, seeing that all who are born into this world are born into it having a sin debt, owing their very lives to pay that debt, He says and has said to us, believe in My Son and be saved. Turn from your sin and repent and I will forgive your sin debt in full. I want you to note again, this cost God something. Someone had to pay the debt. Just because we don't have to pay it, the debt still remained. But God through Jesus took the loss. He gave His only Son to die as payment for our debt.

With all of this in mind, how should we be when it comes to forgiving others? The servant who was forgiven the great debt of ten thousand talents didn't handle it so well. Scripture says that he went and found one of his fellow servants who owed him a fraction of what he owed the king. He actually grabbed his fellow servant by the throat and said, "Pay me what you owe!" The fellow servant did exactly what he had done before the king and fell down at his feet and begged him to be patient, that he would pay all, but he would not be patient and had him thrown in prison till he should pay the debt. You know the rest of the parable. The king got wind of it and had the man delivered to the torturers until he should pay all. Before the king did this though, he said to the servant, "You wicked servant! I forgave you all that debt because you begged me. Should you not also have had compassion on your fellow servant, just as I had pity on you?" Indeed, he should have and so should we, remembering the compassion and pity the Lord has had on us through just our salvation experience alone, not to mention all the sin that we have committed and been forgiven of since we were saved.

Jesus finishes the parable explaining how the king had his servant delivered to the torturers until he should pay all that was due to him and then He makes one final statement outside of the parable to Peter and the group He was speaking to. *"So My heavenly Father will do to you if each of you, from his heart, does not forgive his brother his trespass."* Why did Jesus say this? Why did He use the phrase, "From his heart?" Just prior to this starting in **Matthew 18:15** Jesus is instructing the disciples on dealing with a sinning brother and the steps they/we should take. Jesus notes each step to take. 1. Go and tell him his fault between you and him alone. 2. If he will not hear you take one or two with you that by the mouth of two or three witnesses every word may be established. 3. If he refuses to hear them, tell it to the church. 4. If he refuses to hear the church, let him be to you as a heathen or a tax collector. Four steps, a formula if you will, given by Jesus in dealing with one who has sinned against you. Knowing this, it makes sense why Peter would then ask Jesus, "How often shall my brother sin against me and I forgive him? Up to seven times?" Peter asks Jesus a great question here especially after Jesus just explained how to deal with someone who has sinned against you. Jesus tells him to forgive not just seven times, but seventy times seven. Peter seems to be asking for another step concerning forgiveness in this whole line of instruction from Jesus, but then Jesus tells the parable and makes perfectly clear that forgiveness is not just another step in this process. Jesus points out in the parable that when the servant began to beg the king that the king was moved with compassion for him and forgave the debt. The king didn't ask for the royal scroll with a list of how many times he had given the servant more time to pay that he might say, "I have forgiven this man three times for missing his payment. He has four more times and then off to prison with him." No, he had compassion on him and forgave the debt completely. You see forgiveness, even though we are commanded to forgive one another is never to be seen as just something that you have to do. Jesus tells us here at the end of the parable that it must be something that is moved by compassion in the heart.

What does this look like? When I sin against someone it creates a debt. In a perfect situation I should go to them and apologize. The scriptures say in *Matthew 5:23-26 "Therefore if you bring your gift to the altar, and there remember that your brother has something against you, "leave your gift there before the altar, and go your way. First be reconciled to your brother, and then come and offer your gift. "Agree with your adversary quickly, while you are on the way with him, lest your adversary deliver you to the judge, the judge hand you over to the officer, and you be thrown into prison. "Assuredly, I say to you, you will by no means get out of there till you have paid the last penny."* When I forgive someone, I mean forgive them from the heart, I release them from that debt. Look at Stephen in *Acts 7:59-60*. While he was being stoned by the crowd, he cried out with a loud voice, *"Lord, do not charge them with this sin."* Stephen, had forgiven them from the heart. He had released them from the debt they owed for murdering him, even crying to the Lord, do not charge them with this sin!

Have you ever heard someone say, "I forgive you, but I will never forget what you have done?" Would you call that, "Forgiving from the heart?" Granted, you may not forget things that people have done to you, but when your heart is set on not forgetting those things, are you really forgiving from the heart? Are you really releasing them from that debt? Let me remind you that God, who is our example, said in *Jeremiah 31:34* concerning the house of Israel, ***"For I will forgive their iniquity, and their sin I will remember no more."*** If we are to forgive from the heart, then from the heart we are to release them from any sin debt toward us. Even if we may not be able to remove from our minds what they have done, at the very least we should never remember it against them as a debt not paid, but settled in full by us through forgiveness from a heart of compassion and pity.

One final thought. We all know what is called, "The Lord's Prayer." It is not actually the Lord's prayer, but more of an outline from Jesus of how we should pray.

> ***Our Father which art in heaven, Hallowed be Thy name. Thy kingdom come. Thy will be done in earth, as it is in heaven. Give us this day our daily bread and forgive us our debts, as we forgive our debtors. And lead us not into temptation, but deliver us from evil: For Thine is the kingdom, and the power, and the glory, forever. Amen***

> ***Mathew 6:9-13***

Jesus says in this outline or framework for how to pray, forgive us our debts as we forgive our debtors. In some translations it says, forgive us our trespasses as we forgive those who trespass against us. If you will notice, this is the only portion of the outline that is conditional upon our action. Forgive us our debts AS we forgive our debtors. Jesus is actually directing us in that we should pray for forgiveness, but also teaching us that our forgiveness from the Father is conditional upon us forgiving others. That is heavy! You mean to tell me that if I am unforgiving toward people then the Lord will be unforgiving toward me? Yes! That is exactly what I am saying. And Jesus spells it out clearly in **Matthew 6:14-15** right after the outline for the prayer He just gave.

For if you forgive men their trespasses,
Your heavenly Father will also forgive you.
But if you do not forgive men their trespasses, neither
will your Father forgive
your trespasses.

It is interesting how Jesus reiterates this part of His outline on how we should pray and this part only. How serious do you think Jesus is about forgiveness? Specifically, us forgiving others?

My fellow servants, to forgive must come from the heart. It must come from a heart of compassion, through love and forgiveness with an honest and humble realization of who you are and what the Father has forgiven you of. This will put a spear right through the heart of bitterness. Remember, thankfulness creates a depth of wisdom and compassion, that leads to forgiving and loving others. YOU will then be free to have peace without a bitter heart.

8

The Healing of God

He heals the broken hearted
and binds up their wounds.
Psalm 147:3

God wants you to be healed...

Whether it is bitterness from being hurt deeply, envy, loss, or even being done dirty, whatever the cause is, you need to be healed. You also need to look at bitterness as being sin. Call it what it is. Being bitter in heart goes directly against God and His word, and you must see it that way. God knows your deepest and most inner thoughts and feelings. He has all of your ways spread out before Him like a fan or like a puzzle when you lay all the pieces out on the table, flip them over and then spread them out so you can get all the edge pieces. David tells us this in *Psalm 139:1-3*

O LORD, You have searched me and known me. You know my sitting down and my rising up; You understand

my thought afar off. You comprehend my path and my lying down, And are acquainted with all my ways.

With God knowing you so intimately this way, who better to get direction from? I love the fact that God is not just this all knowing supreme being who because of His sovereignty just happens to know everything about us. While God is The All Knowing, Sovereign Creator of all things, David, moved by the Spirit of God, says of Him, "You have searched me and known me." Ahhhh, how beautiful it is, to know that the God of all the universe and everything that is in it, has taken the time to search into and know each and every one of us. He knows all the fine details of you and I. Even the hairs on your head are all numbered. ***Matthew 10:29-30*** He collects all your tears and puts them in a bottle. ***Psalm 56:8*** He knows your sitting down and your rising up. He knows which specific path you will take in every event of life. He even knows what your sleep is like when you lie down. Do you know that because of His foreknowledge, He knows our thoughts before we even think them?

With all of these things being the way they are, God also sees all the mistakes in our thinking. He sees all the wrong decisions we will make ahead of time concerning what path we choose to take in any given event of life. He sees all the hurt that will come to us and what path we will choose because of that hurt. He sees the paths we will choose because of the flesh, pride, anger, jealousy, covetousness, envy, fleshly desires, and the like. God doesn't see all just because He's God. It is because He loves us that He searches us and knows all that we are. With this foreknowledge God possesses, it makes this next set of verses so incredibly important to our lives.

Proverbs 3:5-6

> **Trust in the Lord with all of your heart, and lean not on your own understanding. In all your ways acknowledge Him and He shall direct your paths.**

With the Lord having all our ways, all the paths that we will choose in life in every circumstance, laid out before Him, can you see His great and awesome love for us in telling us to trust in Him?!?! Then He says, "lean not on your own understanding," meaning, I have all your paths laid out before Me. I see the one you will take when that person slanders your name. You will choose the wrong path, so trust in Me and not in yourself. I have used slander in this instance to draw the picture for you, but you can put any negative thing that has been done to you in that place. God already knows the path you are going to take in your reaction to what has been done to you and it may be the wrong one. Many believers, have gotten to this point in life in different situations where something wrong had been done to them and they didn't stop to ask the Lord how to deal with it. Many have gotten to this point and knew what path the Lord was directing them on but chose not to follow the Lord. The rest of the verse does say, "In all your ways acknowledge Him and He shall direct your paths." Isn't it great that the God of the universe says to you, If you will just sit down and take a moment to talk to Me about what is going on in your life and how to handle it, I will show you the correct path to take? Do you do that? Do you take all your cares to the Lord and let Him sort them out for you? *1Peter 5:7* tells us *to cast our care upon the Lord for He cares for us.* And in *Psalm 55:22* it says, *"Cast your burden upon the Lord and He shall sustain you; He shall never permit the righteous to be moved."*

There is an app you can get on your phone and it will literally direct your path. HaHa!!! Don't we wish? There really is an app though, that you can get on your phone for travel purposes. You punch in where you want to go and it will give you real time updates and change the directions (path) on the fly to get you to your desired destination as quickly and as safely as possible. There are millions who use and trust this app to get them to their destination without running into traffic or accidents. Why will we be so quick to trust something man has made, but be so hesitant or unwilling to trust the One who has created man?

If we are talking about God's healing, why did I just spell all of this out? Because clearly, God's heart is to keep us from having things in our life that we need to be healed of. I have noticed over the years that a lot of the heartache in my life came from my own choices. Whereas, if I had acknowledged the Lord in all my ways, He would have shown me which way to go, what path to take, and I would not have had to go through all the heartache that

I did. Can you relate to that last statement in any way? Sometimes heartache is thrust upon us and it is not our fault, but sometimes it is because of the choices we have made. Whichever the case, God wants us to be whole. God wants to heal us.

I think it is so cool to hear of God's reaction to a sinning nation who will turn to Him.

> *"I will heal their backsliding, I will love them freely, For My anger has turned away from him. I will be like the dew to Israel; He shall grow like the lily, And lengthen his roots like Lebanon. His branches shall spread; His beauty shall be like an olive tree, And his fragrance like Lebanon. Those who dwell under his shadow shall return; They shall be revived like grain, And grow like a vine. Their scent shall be like the wine of Lebanon.*

> *Hosea 14:4-7*

You may need more healing than you think. Possibly, you may first need healing for what has been done to you. Secondly, and this damage is almost always worse, you need to be healed from all that bitterness and sin has caused in your heart and mind. In the previous verse, God said that He would heal their backsliding. That is, backsliding from a righteous standing before God into the old person you used to be before the Lord came into your life. You remember, where it wasn't even a second thought to cut someone out of your life and hold a grudge against them, like forever. However, most of the time it was over a really good reason like, they made a snide remark about the way your gravy tasted at Thanksgiving last year, or maybe you didn't get invited to watch the game with everyone else. You know, really important life changing things.

Yes, that last bit was a joke, but you know that those actual scenarios have played out and people are hurt and jacked up over things just like that. Whatever it is that has gotten you to a place where you are bitter you need to be healed and only God can do that in your life. The word says, *"For the wages of sin is death, but the gift of God is eternal life in Christ Jesus our Lord." Romans 6:23* Now, this we know to be true, but on the way to that death, sin wreaks havoc in a life. It destroys the goodness of the Holy Spirit in a person. It destroys relationships. It destroys understanding. It bypasses and has no time for wisdom. Sin will literally steal the life out of the living while they yet breathe. And for all this, the Lord says...

> *"Return you backsliding children And I will heal your backslidings."*
>
> *Jeremiah 3:22*
>
> *For I will restore health to you And heal you of your wounds,' says the LORD,*

'Because they called you an outcast saying: "This is Zion; No one seeks her."

Jeremiah 30:17

'Behold, I will bring it health and healing; I will heal them and reveal to them the abundance of peace and truth. 'And I will cause the captives of Judah and the captives of Israel to return, and will rebuild those places as at the first. 'I will cleanse them from all their iniquity by which they have sinned against Me, and I will pardon all their iniquities by which they have sinned and by which they have transgressed against Me. 'Then it shall be to Me a name of joy, a praise, and an honor before all nations of the earth, who shall hear all the good that I do to them; they shall fear and tremble for all the goodness and all the prosperity that I provide for it.'

Jeremiah 33:6-9

If you haven't been healed by the Lord from the bitterness in your heart or you don't think He can heal you, it is only because you are not willing. God is more than willing to heal you. It is His desire to heal you. And not only to heal your hurt, but to heal all that sin has done in your life by not following Him in every way. I would like to say as I have said earlier, I know that there are deep hurts in some people's lives. Abuse that has been thrust upon them in one fashion or another. God knows the depths of all that has been done to you. He also knows the path that you have taken to deal with those things. He also is the God of tender mercies, ready to heal, ready to breathe joyful life into an otherwise seemingly life of continual sorrow. I am not a doctor of any sort, but I know my God. He heals to the uttermost, to the depths of wherever you are and passed that. My God is the only one who brings back what man carelessly destroys. He makes the heartache a thing in the past, overcome by His great love and compassion. PLEASE, come to the Lord and see that He is generous with His great love and healing.

One of the greatest obstacles I have seen with people in being healed by the Lord from bitterness, is themselves. I have watched the Lord reach His hand out to people to bring healing into their life only to watch them bat His hand away. Pride, selfishness, not wanting to let go of your way will stop you from allowing God to heal you. When you see God in the old testament reaching out to the children of Israel that He might heal them and their land and restore them, it is always in conjunction with repentance. I believe there is also another reason people don't let God heal the heart and soul. It is very possibly that the event that caused them so much pain, they have buried in an attempt to cope with life and have some sort of peace, only that is not peace. For God to heal the heart and soul it may take remembering those hurts and events all over again. Some are terrified over this prospect. If I may encourage you. You can trust God. He made you. He knows how to deliver you and He knows how to bring you to a place where there is true peace with nothing buried. It is well worth going back over some hurtful memories just for a little bit with the Lord that you may be set free forever from the pain and the bitterness that came from miss-handling the issue to begin with.

To assist in all of this, you must shoot straight with yourself. There is an ancient Greek saying, "Know thyself." This is what I get from this saying. Be honest with yourself. Don't try to deceive yourself into thinking you are something that you are not or vice-versa. Don't try to deceive yourself into thinking that you're not something that you actually are. If you have a problem with lying you will never overcome lying by acting like you don't have a problem with it, when you get caught in it over and over again. Be honest with yourself. You must be able to say to yourself, if I get in a bind, I am the kind of person who will lie to get out of it. AND I NEED YOU FATHER TO HELP ME NOT DO THIS ANYMORE. This is where God will meet you and deliver you. Until that point, He will be chastening you. Because God loves you and wants you to be whole, he will chasten you. Remember in **Revelation 3:19** He said, *"As many as I love, I rebuke and chasten. Therefore be zealous and repent."* You won't get away with it! You will not get away with sin, because God loves you. I used lying for the scenario here, but you can and should put in whatever you have. It could be pride, gossip, lust, alcohol, envy, jealousy, self-seeking, whatever it may be, shoot straight with yourself and be honest. God already knows it and most all of your family and friends probably know it as well.

What's going on in your life right now? Are you at odds with people? Has God been speaking to you, telling you to turn from the path you are on and you are just not listening? Is the Holy Spirit convicting you but you are just stubbornly hanging on to your fleshly heart no matter what He says? Why are you doing that? Have you come to God to get your will accomplished? That is another book altogether. Really though, who comes to God so they can be miserable their whole life because they are not getting their way?

A Sober Talk About God's Grace

Many of you may be asking, "What about grace?" Where does grace fit in to all of this? Maybe you are saying to yourself, "God knows this is just the way I am. He knows my heart though. I'm standing in His grace." Let me please say to you, "I don't think that means what you think that means." Firstly, and this is for all of us, a heart without Jesus, is a deceitful and desperately wicked heart. *Jeremiah 17:9* And you might say, "but I am a believer." Please note this: Anytime you are operating in the flesh, even as a believer, you are operating from a heart that is deceitful and desperately wicked. Anytime you are operating in the Spirit, you are operating from a heart that has been moved by the Spirit of God to crucify the flesh and follow God.

Grace does not cover sin. Jesus takes away sin. The Greek word for grace is "Charis" and it means good-will, loving kindness, FAVOR. You will hear it said that "Charis" means unmerited favor, and while the favor of God is unmerited as also everything else from God except for the wages of sin *Romans 6:23*, we deserve death, the word Charis simply means, favor.

Now, put your seatbelts on as we look at the grace (favor) of God in our lives!

For the law was given through Moses, but GRACE and truth came through Jesus Christ.

John 1:17 God has given His grace (favor) to us through Jesus Christ.

Through Him we receive GRACE and apostleship for obedience to the faith among all nations for His name. *Romans 1:5* We have received grace (favor) from God to help us to be obedient to the faith.

In Him we have redemption through His blood, the forgiveness of sins, according to the riches of His GRACE. *Ephesians 1:7* It is the riches of Jesus' grace (favor) toward us that He would shed His blood as payment for our sin.

To me who am less that the least of all the saints, this GRACE was given, that I should preach among the Gentiles the unsearchable riches of Christ. Ephesians 3:8

It is the grace (favor) of God toward us that we should be given gifts to use as fellow workers with Christ.

You therefore, my son, be strong in the GRACE that is in Christ Jesus. 2Timothy 2:1 We are to be strong in the grace (favor) that is in Christ Jesus. Meaning, trust it, depend on it.

For the GRACE of God that brings salvation has appeared to all men, teaching us that, denying ungodliness and worldly lust, we should live soberly, righteously, and godly in this present age. Titus 2:11-12 God's grace (favor) not only has brought salvation to us, but also teaches us how to walk uprightly.

Let us therefore come boldly to the throne of GRACE, that we may obtain mercy and find GRACE to help in time of need. Hebrews 4:16

Let's stop right there. Listen, if you know that you are bitter towards someone or some situation, I want you to stop and take in the depth of this verse. Let us therefore come boldly to the throne of grace (favor). Do you know what that means? The verse before it says, *For we do not have a High Priest who cannot sympathize with our weaknesses, but was in all points tempted as we are, yet without sin. Hebrews 4:15* This means first of all that Jesus was tempted just as we are, and though He never fell and was and is without sin, He still knows the depths of the difficulty it will take for us to crucify the flesh and not sin. With this in mind, the scripture says, *"Let us therefore come boldly."* Let us run to the throne of grace (favor) without hesitation, knowing that my Jesus, my Papa, is sitting there just waiting to help me! It then says, ***That we may obtain mercy and find grace to help in time of need.*** He is waiting to direct, He is waiting to forgive, He is waiting to restore, He is waiting to heal the broken hearted and bind up all your wounds. Please, let Him do this in your life today. His grace (favor) is for you!

Do you ever wonder why most of Jesus' miracles were of healing, making people whole, even to the point of casting out demons and raising people from the dead? I mean, He is God. He could have turned the sky purple for an afternoon. He could have brought the sun so close to the earth that they could have touched it without harm. He could have created an automobile so that they didn't have to walk everywhere. The list is endless of what He could have done, but mostly all that He did was heal people. With lovely compassion, being personal with the people, meeting them where they were in life, He healed them and made them whole. Let's look at some.

Matthew 8:1-4 Jesus cleanses a man with leprosy.

Matthew 8:5-13 Jesus heals a centurion's paralyzed servant in Capernaum.

Matthew 8:14-15 Jesus heals Peter's mother-in-law.

Matthew 8:16-17 Jesus heals many sick and oppressed at evening.

Matthew 8:28-33 Jesus casts the demons out of two men in the tombs.

Matthew 9:1-8 Jesus heals a paralytic lying on a bed.

Matthew 9:18, 23-26 Jesus raises Jairus' daughter back to life.

Matthew 9:20-22 Jesus heals a woman in the crowd with an issue of blood.

Matthew 9:27-31 Jesus heals two blind men.

Matthew 9:32-34 Jesus heals a man who was unable to speak.

Matthew 12:9-14 Jesus heals a man's withered hand on the sabbath.

Matthew 12:22-23 Jesus heals a blind, mute demoniac.

Matthew 14:34-36 Jesus heals many sick in Gennesaret as they touch His garment.

Matthew 15:21-28 Jesus heals a Gentile woman's demon possessed daughter.

Matthew 17:14-20 Jesus heals a boy with an unclean spirit.

Matthew 20:29-34 Jesus restores sight to two men.

Mark 1:21-27 Jesus drives out an evil spirit from a man in Capernaum.

Mark 2:1-5 Jesus heals a paralytic lowered down through the roof.

Mark 7:31-37 Jesus heals a deaf and dumb man.

Mark 8:22-26 Jesus heals a blind man at Bethsaida.

Luke 7:11-17 Jesus raises a widow's son from the dead in Nain.

Luke 13:10-17 Jesus heals a woman who had been crippled for eighteen years.

Luke 14:1-6 Jesus heals a man with dropsy on the sabbath.

Luke 17:11-19 Jesus cleanses ten lepers on the way to Jerusalem.

Luke 22:50-51 Jesus heals a servant's severed ear while He is being arrested.

John 4:46-54 Jesus heals a nobleman's son at Capernaum in Galilee.

John 5:1-15 Jesus heals an invalid at Bethesda.

John 9:1-12 Jesus heals a man born blind.

John 11:1-45 Jesus raises Lazarus from the dead in Bethany.

Besides these, there are only nine other recorded miracles of Jesus in all four gospels. The others range from feeding the five thousand to walking on water, and from turning the water into wine to pulling the temple tax out of a fish's mouth. This says a lot about the character of Jesus in that He was way more concerned about the well-being of people than He was anything else. Scripture tells us in **Hebrews 13:8 Jesus Christ is the same yesterday, today, and forever.** And in **Malachi 3:6** it says, **I am the LORD, I do not change;** Jesus' heart is the same today as it was then and He can heal your broken heart. He can heal your backsliding. He can heal you of all bitterness. He can heal the years of a tainted spirit because of bitterness. You just have to let Him. I want you to know, that the receiving of this kind of healing from God is always YES! If you ask God to heal you and you let Him heal you and you follow Him, HE WILL HEAL YOU. This is not like a disease where sometimes the Lord heals and sometimes, He chooses not to. We just read through several verses of Jesus healing many people physically, and life has shown us that Jesus does not heal everyone who has a physical ailment. One thing though, you can always count on, is that Jesus is ready, willing, and oh so able, to heal any and all effects to the mind, heart, soul from sin. **Isaiah 53:5** says, **and by His stripes we are healed** and that is a guarantee, an absolute. If you call upon the Lord, He will not only save you from the power of sin, but he will also heal you from the effects of the power of sin. Sin in the heart of man makes him sick. It makes man rotten inside. *James 1:15* says, *sin, when it is full grown brings forth death.* Jesus, who is called The Great Physician has the compassion, heart, and desire to truly heal. In Matthew chapter nine Jesus is sitting with tax collectors and sinners and when the Pharisee's saw it they asked the disciples, why does He do that? When Jesus heard that, He said to them, *Those who are well have no need of a physician, but those who are sick." "But go learn what this means: 'I desire mercy and not sacrifice. For I did not come to call the righteous, but sinners, to repentance. Matthew 9:12-13*

If you are bitter in heart or in sin of any sort, you are spiritually sick and need The Great Physician, Jesus to heal you and make you whole again. Don't wait! Jesus' heart was to sit right in the middle of where the people needed to be healed so He could do just that, heal them. Let Him heal you, Let Him deliver you, that you might be whole and your joy filled up and overflowing!!!!!

9

Repentance

So, here we are. We've learned a lot of things in just a little bit of time. What has God been speaking to your heart? Have you been convicted? The real question is, if there is conviction, are you listening? Are you softening your heart? Have the scriptures in this book spoken to you that it might soften your heart? You know, one thing about bitterness is that it hardens the heart. But God's grace (favor) toward us is to lead us back to Him. Scripture tells us *it's God's goodness that leads us to repentance.* I love what the actual verse says. In its context it is speaking to those who judge another for doing the very thing that they also do. Paul asks them, do you think you will escape the judgement of God? Then he says this to them,

Or do you despise the riches of His goodness, forbearance, and longsuffering, not knowing that the goodness of God leads you to repentance? Romans 2:4

The word 'despise' in the Greek is 'kataphroneo' and it means to think little or nothing of.

The word 'forbearance' in the Greek is 'anoche' and it means toleration.

The word 'longsuffering' in the Greek is 'makrothymia' and means patience.

Remember, we just spoke a bunch about shooting straight with yourself. So, here is your opportunity to practice it. Be honest with yourself.

Where is your heart right now? Do you think little or nothing of the riches of God's goodness, toleration of your bitterness, while He patiently waits for you to turn to Him and repent, even as it is His goodness, His gracious filled heart toward you that leads you to that very repentance that He might make you whole and righteous? Let me ask this another way. What value do you put on the fact that God who is rich in mercy and abundant in grace (favor) toward you, is leading you to repent of the very sin which is against Him, that He might forgive you, heal you of sin, and restore you in righteous? What value do you place on that? If you are gauging your value on how you emotionally feel about it, stop. The value of this is priceless. The scriptures say, the wages of sin is death and God's goodness is to lead you away from that death and into life. The emotion can come after the fact and should, from a grateful heart, but how you value it should come at face value. This is a good deal, people!!! We would be crazy to think little of or miss the value of this grace (favor) given to us by God.

I always like to say that whenever the word of God is being spoken and explained to people, God is speaking to those very people. I am confident that there is enough of God's word in this book that if you took all of my words out, scripture alone would convict the soul of those who will listen. If you are reading this book, God is speaking to you. And I would say, LISTEN TO HIM. Dear Saint, repent. Turn from your ways and back to the ways of God. Let a time of refreshing come over you from the Lord through repentance as you let all of that bitterness go, choosing to forgive and love those who have sinned against you. Choose to forgive from the heart and love deeply!

The Road Before Me

Repentance in the life of a believer must be constant. Not one of us has or ever will reach a place where we are permanently without sin on this earth. As a matter of fact, scripture tells us in *1John 1:8 If we say we have no sin, we deceive ourselves, and the truth is not in us.* Having said that, we should be sinning less the longer we walk with the Lord. God wants you to grow in His righteousness. Since change in the believer's life comes through the word of God by the power of the Holy Spirit, ever growing in the knowledge of the word of God is vital to the Christian life. We see this in *Matthew 4:4 Man shall not live by bread alone but by every word that proceeds from the mouth of God,* and again in *Romans 12:1-2 Do not be conformed to this world, but be transformed by the renewing of your mind.* The renewing of your mind comes from reading God's word. *Also, James 1:21 says, Therefore lay aside all filthiness and overflow of wickedness, and receive with meekness the implanted word, which is able to save your souls.* You must stay in the Word! Let's see what the scriptures tell us about King David's encounter with sin. *How can a young man cleanse his way? By taking heed according to Your word. With my whole heart I have sought You; Oh, let me not wander from Your commandments! Your word I have hidden in my heart, that I might not sin against You.* **Psalm 119:9-11**

In the previous verse we see David making the statement or posing the question, "How can a young man cleans his way?" How can someone who is caught up in sin, cleans his way, get out of sin? He actually answers this right along with the question and it is a very short and simple answer. "By taking heed according to your word." This is one of the first verses that I memorized years ago. This verse set a standard in my life and should be the standard for every believer's life. Why a standard, because sin is always a reality the believer will have to deal with in this life. It will never be something, in this life, where we can say, 'ok, glad that's done with. Now we can just cruise.' We will always have the flesh fighting to come back to life and we will always have satan tempting us to sin against God. Since this is the case, there must be a standard kept in place by us by which we keep our flesh dead (crucified) and we guard ourselves from falling into temptation.

The answer to David's question of how a young man cleanses his way was this; "By taking heed to Your word." That is God's word. This phrase, "Taking heed" in the Hebrew means to keep or observe. Basically, it means to DO. So, we could read the verse like this, How can a young man cleans his way? By doing (obeying) Your word. Then David goes even further with this idea and he says in verse 11, "Your word I have hidden in my heart, that I might not sin against You." Now, follow the thought process here, David first asks, How can a young man cleans his way? Answer: By taking heed according to Your word. So, the question is, how can a man who is already in sin cleanse his way. David thinks ahead here that if the fact is that by obeying Your word I can cleans my way, then I will hide Your word in my heart so that I don't sin against You in the first place, thus keeping my way clean.

Let me explain to you how David's plan works. You see in *John 14:26* the word of God says that the Holy Spirit will bring all things to your remembrance that Jesus said to you. What this means to us today is that as we are reading and studying our Bible we are learning about God, Jesus, and the Holy Spirit. We are also learning how to walk with God. We are learning verses of scripture that will transform us by renewing of our minds. As we are doing this, here comes temptation. Maybe someone has cut you off while driving and immediately you are tempted to start cussing that person out. Your anger is boiling over, but at that moment, the Holy Spirit brings to your remembrance *Ephesians 4:26 Be angry and do not*

sin. And **1Corinthians 13:4-7 Love suffers long, love is not provoked.** Or how about **Ephesians 4:29 or Colossians 3:8** which both instruct us not to cuss. This is partially what David is speaking about here. He says, "Your word I have hidden in my heart that I might not sin against you." Meaning firstly, I am already training myself according to Your word so that my old character is killed off (crucified). I have been walking in Your word so that I am not so easily tempted, but also since I have been doing that and keeping Your word in my heart by meditating on it, praying about the understanding of it, and memorizing it, the Holy Spirit is faithful to bring that word right back to my mind when tempted to keep me from falling into temptation.

All of this to say, Repent. Why should you live out a bitter life of any sort, having become defiled by bitterness, only to get to the end and realize, there is no place found for you in heaven, but an even greater bitterness lived out for eternity in the Lake of Fire?

Speaking of the New Jerusalem in **Revelation 21:27**

> **But there shall by no means enter it anything that defiles, or causes an abomination or a lie, but only those who are written in the Lamb's Book of Life.**

God's heart is that you not be defiled through bitterness, but that you live and be with Him both now and forever. His grace (favor) is for you. His goodness leads you to repentance. Repent now, and live!

10

Salvation

If you prayed the prayer and answered the call back in chapter three, You are Saved!!! As God's word tells us in **John 5:24**, you have **passed from death into life**. You will not go to hell when you die, but you will go to be with the Lord, entering His rest and have peace forever.

There is a transformation that God wants to do in your life starting today! Since God is the one who created you, He is the only one who can show you how to live this life to the fullest and bring you to a place where you have the qualities of **love, joy, peace, long-suffering, kindness, goodness, faithfulness, gentleness, and self-control. Galatians 5:22-23**.

You will find God's plan for this transformation of your life in the Bible. This is why getting a Bible and spending time in it daily is one of the most important things you must do now. The Bible tells us all about who God is and who Jesus is. It is so vast in its wisdom it will even tell you who you are, if you are willing to read and believe. **Hebrews 4:12-13**.

When you believed in Jesus you received the Holy Spirit of God. *John 14:26*. As you read God's word (The Bible), the Holy Spirit will bring back to your memory those things that you have read at an important time in life when you need it. The Holy Spirit will also convict you of sin. *John 16:8-11*. This means that from this point on when you sin against God, His Holy Spirit will speak to you immediately, calling you to turn from that sin, to stop and repent and ask for forgiveness. Always be sure to thank the Lord for forgiving you, because if you ask with an honest heart for forgiveness, He will surely forgive you and restore you in righteousness! As you begin to listen and become more familiar with the Holy Spirit speaking to you in your spirit, you will hear His conviction before you sin that you might not fall into sin at all.

The Bible tells us in Genesis chapter three how Adam and Eve ate the fruit of the tree of the knowledge of good and evil. This is the tree that God told them not to eat of. He told them that the day they ate of that tree they would die. Well, they ate of it and they didn't drop dead. So, what was the deal? Before they ate of the tree they belonged to God and were of the same Spirit with Him, but when they disobeyed God and ate the fruit that He commanded them not to, they died a spiritual death and no longer were they of the same Spirit of God. They no longer belonged to Him. Further judgement would mean a physical death one day.

Now the scriptures say in **Romans 6:23** that **the wages of sin is death.** I want you to think of this in the terms of hiring someone for a job. If you needed a roof put on your house you might ask, what does a roofer cost? What will I need to pay him to put a roof on my house? What are his wages? Now we see that sin charges death to be in your life. That is the death of your soul, condemned to hell. However, the later part of this verse says, ***the gift of God is eternal life in Christ Jesus our Lord***. So, sin demands payment, even the death of your soul, but God gives life freely through Jesus Christ. Since sin must receive the wage of death, for there is no free sin, the Bible says that sin must be paid for with blood. ***Leviticus 17:11 says, The life of the flesh is in the blood, and it is blood that is required to make atonement for the soul.*** God knowing this and loving mankind, sent His Son, Jesus Christ to die on a cross and shed His blood as payment for the sin of the world. One time for all. So, if you believe in Jesus as you have, and believe that He is the Son of God and believe in His work on the cross to make the required payment for sin, then you are saved! Jesus Christ has paid your sin debt. He has paid the wages for your sin in FULL!

What a blessing this is! You are now in the family of God! Walk with him every day. Read your Bible every day. Find a good Bible teaching church. Go get fed the word of God and make new friendships with people who are avidly seeking the Lord and walking with Him.

Will you please share this story of salvation with everyone you are able to?

My hope and prayer for you is that you will draw so close to God, that every step you take and every word you speak will be led by Him. Continue with the Lord, no matter what.

He has you in His hand…

> *"My sheep hear My voice, and I know them, and they follow Me. "And I give them eternal life, and they shall never perish; neither shall anyone snatch them out of My hand. "My Father, who has given them to Me, is greater than all; and no one is able to snatch them out of My Father's hand. "I and My Father are one."*
>
> *John 10:27-28*

Printed in the United States
By Bookmasters